DELICIOUS $5 DINNERS

Easy Meals for Any Night of the Week!

HAYSTACK MEDIA
SAN DIEGO, CA

Cover image: shutterstock 129147323, p. 37: shutterstock 102399499 p.56: shutterstock 72312247

Cover & Interior Design: Kayla Blanco | All other photography: Haystack Media

Published in the United States of America by

HAYSTACK MEDIA
SAN DIEGO, CA

ISBN: 978-1-929862-11-5

10   9   8   7   6   5   4   3   2   1

TABLE OF CONTENTS

Savory Ham & Cheese Galette

SERVES 6 TO 8

Easy, yet elegant enough for guests!

1 T. extra virgin olive oil

½ c. fresh mushrooms, sliced

½ yellow onion, peeled, thinly sliced

1 large zucchini, cut in ¼-inch slices

1 t. dried thyme

salt and pepper to taste

1 prepared pastry crust

¼ lb. smoked ham, diced

½ c. Monterey Jack cheese, shredded

1 T. milk

Preheat the oven to 400°F. In a skillet, heat the oil and sauté the mushrooms, onion and zucchini until soft. Add the thyme, salt and pepper and continue cooking until vegetables are tender-crisp. Roll or pat the pastry into a 9 inch circle and place on a baking sheet. Spoon the mixture into the center of the pie crust, leaving a 1-inch border on the edges. Top with the ham and cheese. Fold the pastry edges toward the center to partially cover the top of the filling. Crimp the pastry edges and brush with milk. Bake 25-30 minutes until golden.

Roasted Sweet Potato Salad with Turkey & Wild Rice

SERVES 4

A main dish worthy of a warm summer evening, this salad is best when served chilled. Serve with rolls and market greens.

One Dish Meals

2 c. sweet potato, peeled, cut into 1-inch cubes

1 T. extra virgin olive oil

¼ t. salt

1 clove garlic, minced

1 c. cooked turkey, diced

7 oz. box wild rice blend, prepared as directed

¼ c. carrots, shredded

¼ c. celery, chopped

3 T. red onion, finely chopped

¼ c. white wine vinegar

2 T. extra virgin olive oil

1 t. soy sauce

½ t. ground black pepper

Preheat the oven to 375°F. Place the sweet potato cubes on a baking sheet. Toss with the olive oil, salt and garlic. Roast for 30-35 minutes, turning once, until potatoes are tender. Remove and cool. In a large mixing bowl, combine the potatoes, turkey, rice blend, carrots, celery and onion. Stir to mix well. Sprinkle the vinegar, olive oil, soy sauce and pepper over all. Toss. Taste and adjust seasonings. Chill before serving.

Chicken, Kale & Parmesan Risotto

SERVES 6

Choose bright, fresh kale and, when possible, use freshly grated Parmesan cheese.

4 c. chicken broth

1 T. extra virgin olive oil

½ c. yellow onion, diced

1 clove garlic, minced

1½ c. Arborio rice

½ c. Parmesan cheese, freshly grated, plus more for garnish

1 c. cooked chicken, shredded into bite-sized pieces

1 c. fresh kale, steamed and chopped

Heat the broth in a saucepan and keep warm. In a skillet, heat the olive oil and add the onion and garlic. Sauté 2 to 3 minutes. Add the rice to the onion and stir. Reduce the heat to low and add 1 cup of the broth, stirring slowly until the broth is absorbed, about 8 minutes. Continue adding broth, 1 cup at a time, stirring each time until the liquid is absorbed. When ready, add the chicken, kale, cheese, salt and pepper to taste. Stir and adjust seasonings. Add broth if mixture is too thick. Garnish with additional cheese, if desired. Serves 6.

Tex-Mex Salsa Beef Skillet

SERVES 4

1 lb. lean ground beef

16 oz. prepared salsa

15 oz. can black beans, drained

1 c. long grain white rice, uncooked

1½ c. water

¼ c. green pepper, chopped

1½ c. cheddar cheese, shredded

4 c. tortilla chips

Brown the beef in a large skillet and drain excess grease. Layer the salsa, beans, rice, water and pepper over the beef. Cover and simmer for 25 minutes on low heat.

Spread the cheese over the beef mixture and cook, uncovered, until melted.

Place 1 cup chips in the bottom of each of 4 bowls and spoon the salsa beef over the chips.

One Dish Meals

6

Southern Eggs Creole

Tender vegetables combine with protein-filled eggs for a delicious low-cost supper solution.

¾ c. butter, melted, divided

4 T. all-purpose flour, divided

1 c. whole or lowfat milk

1 t. Worcestershire sauce

salt and pepper to taste

6 hard cooked eggs, peeled and chopped

1 green pepper, coarsely chopped

1 large yellow onion, peeled, chopped

15 oz. can diced tomatoes, with juices

½ t. dried thyme

½ t. ground red pepper

½ c. panko crumbs

Preheat the oven to 350°F. Combine ¼ cup butter and 2 tablespoons flour in a saucepan over low heat. Cook and stir for 1 minute. Slowly add the milk and cook until smooth. Add the Worcestershire sauce, salt and pepper to taste and stir. Add the eggs and remove from heat. In a skillet over medium heat, sauté the peppers and onions in 2 tablespoons butter until soft. Add 2 tablespoons flour, stirring well. Add the tomatoes, thyme, red pepper and salt. Coat a 9 x 9-inch baking dish with cooking spray and spoon the egg mixture into the dish. Top with the tomato sauce and cover with panko crumbs. Drizzle the remaining butter over all. Bake for 30 minutes, uncovered.

One Dish Meals

Parisian Chicken Cassoulette

*A rich, dark gravy accompanies protein-packed beans, chicken and ham.
Serve over hot, cooked rice or split baked potatoes.*

3 c. canned navy beans,
liquid reserved

8 oz. large chicken breast,
cut into 1-inch pieces

4 oz. cooked lean ham, cubed

2 carrots, peeled and sliced

1 medium onion, chopped

1 rib celery, sliced

2 T. brown sugar, packed

salt and pepper to taste

½ t. dry mustard

6 oz. can tomato paste

2 T. dark molasses

¼ c. water

Preheat the oven to 350°F. In a 3-quart casserole, combine the beans, chicken, ham, carrots, onions and celery. In a small bowl, mix together the remaining ingredients and blend well. Pour the sauce over the bean mixture and combine. Cover the pan tightly with foil and bake for 45-50 minutes, or until the chicken is completely cooked and the cassoulette is hot.

One Dish Meals

Cheesy Turkey & Spinach Quiche

SERVES 4 TO 6

Familiar flavors combine in a satisfying one-dish dinner.

10 oz. frozen chopped spinach, thawed and drained

1 c. lowfat cottage cheese

4 oz. thin-sliced deli turkey

½ c. Jack cheese, shredded

¼ c. +2 T. Parmesan cheese, grated, divided

¼ c. white onion, chopped

3 eggs, beaten

1 clove garlic, minced

½ t. salt

⅛ t. ground black pepper

1 9-inch prepared pie crust

Preheat the oven to 350°F. In a medium bowl, combine the spinach, cottage cheese, Jack cheese, turkey, 1/4 cup Parmesan cheese, onion, eggs, garlic, salt and pepper, mixing well. Spoon into the crust. Bake, uncovered, for 35 minutes, or until set and lightly browned. Remove, garnish with remaining cheese and cool for 5 minutes before serving.

9

Spicy Manhattan Clam Chowder

Add 1 cup canned navy or black beans to this soup for an additional protein kick.

4 slices bacon, cubed

½ white onion, chopped

½ large carrot, chopped

1 rib celery, chopped

3 large potatoes, peeled, diced

1 c. chicken or vegetable broth

8 oz. diced tomatoes with juices

8 oz. can tomato sauce

1 t. ground black pepper

1 t. seasoned salt

1 t. dried parsley

1 T. hot pepper sauce + more to taste

13 oz. can minced clams with juice

In a stockpot over medium-high heat, fry the bacon until crispy. Add the onions, carrot and celery and sauté for 5 minutes. Add the potatoes, broth, tomatoes with juice, tomato sauce, pepper, salt, parsley and pepper sauce. Bring to a boil, reduce the heat to low and simmer until the potatoes are tender, about 20 minutes. Add the clams and juice. Return the soup to a boil and simmer for 5 minutes. Serves 4.

Homestyle Roast Beef with Root Vegetables

This savory meal is split into two portions to make it both economical and time-saving! Refrigerate and serve the remaining portion within 4 days.

3 lbs. chuck roast

2 t. ground allspice

½ c. + 1 T. all-purpose flour, divided

2 T. canola or vegetable oil

1½ c. beef or vegetable broth

2 T. cider vinegar

2 T. dark molasses

2 t. dry mustard

salt and pepper to taste

3 yellow onions, peeled, thinly sliced

4 large parsnips, peeled, sliced

4 large carrots, peeled, sliced

1 bay leaf

Preheat the oven to 350°F. Press the allspice onto the roast, covering it well. Dredge the roast in ½ cup flour. In a large oven-proof roasting pan over medium-high heat, heat the oil and brown the roast on all sides. Combine the beef broth, vinegar, molasses, mustard andsalt and pepper to taste and pour over the roast. Add the vegetables and bay leaf. Cover tightly and roast for 2 to 2½ hours, until the meat is very tender. Place half of the roast and vegetables on a serving platter. Discard bay leaf. Wrap and refrigerate the remaining portion.

Bring the cooking juices to a boil in the skillet. Whisk 1 tablespoon flour and 1 cup water until smooth. Stir into the juices and simmer on low until thickened. Adjust seasonings and serve with the roast.

One Dish Meals

Baked Potato & Bacon Soup

SERVES 4

Hearty and satisfying. Serve with a leafy salad and whole wheat bread.

3 slices bacon, uncooked

¼ c. celery, chopped

¼ c. carrots, chopped

½ yellow onion, chopped

1 clove garlic, minced

¼ c. all-purpose flour

2½ c. chicken broth

2 large russet potatoes, baked, diced

¾ c. whole milk

¼ c. half and half

salt and pepper to taste

In a stockpot over medium-high heat, fry the bacon until crisp. Remove, crumble and set aside. In the same pot, sauté the celery, carrots, onion and garlic for 2 minutes. Sprinkle the flour over the vegetables and toss to coat. Stir and cook for 2 minutes and whisk in the broth. Continue cooking for 10 to 15 minutes over medium heat, stirring often. Add the potatoes, milk and half and half and stir. Add salt and pepper to taste and simmer on low heat for 10 minutes. Garnish each serving with bacon.

Tender Beef & Vegetable Bowls

*Buy lean cuts of beef, such as round, brisket or rump, to save money.
Cut into bite-sized pieces or shred and slow-cook into tender perfection.*

2 T. extra-virgin olive oil

1 yellow onion, peeled, chopped

1 lb. round steak or stewing beef, cut into 1-inch pieces

1 c. all-purpose flour

salt and pepper to taste

10 oz. can dark beer

3 T. tomato paste

1 t. dried oregano

2 baking potatoes, peeled and quartered

2 c. baby carrots, washed and drained

6 medium white mushrooms, sliced

Heat oil over medium-high heat in a large skillet. Add the onions and sauté until soft. Dredge the meat in the flour; season with salt and pepper. Brown the meat in batches in the pan, adding oil if needed. Add the beer and bring to a simmer, scraping the bits off the bottom. Stir in the paste and oregano. Reduce heat to low, cover tightly and cook until meat is tender, about 1½ to 2 hours. Add the potatoes and carrots during the last hour of cooking; taste and adjust seasonings. Add the mushrooms 15 minutes before serving.

One Dish Meals

Spanish Chicken & Shrimp Paella

SERVES 4

Shrimp doesn't have to be expensive; buy in small quantities and look for frozen medium-sized shrimp for the most economical choice.

2 T. extra virgin olive oil

½ medium onion, peeled, chopped

2 cloves garlic, minced

1 T. fresh parsley, minced

½ t. ground turmeric

2 t. instant chicken bouillon (or use 1 T. concentrated chicken flavoring)

4 oz. chicken breasts, cut into 1-inch pieces

1 green bell pepper, cored, thinly sliced

½ red bell pepper, cored, thinly sliced

8 oz. can tomato sauce

½ t. sugar

salt and pepper to taste

2 c. long grain white rice, uncooked

4 c. water

8 oz. medium shrimp, peeled, with tails on

In a large skillet, sauté the onion, garlic and parsley in the oil for 2 minutes. Add the turmeric and chicken bouillon and stir. Add the chicken and pepper slices and cook over medium heat for 5 minutes. Add the tomato sauce, seasonings, rice and water. Bring to a boil, then reduce the heat to low. Cover and simmer for 10 minutes; add the shrimp. Cover and continue simmering for 10 minutes, until rice is tender and chicken and shrimp are cooked through.

Old World German Beef with Noodles

SERVES 4

A favorite beef dish that complements wide egg noodles perfectly. Serve over cooked brown rice or steamed quinoa for a twist on the traditional.

2 T. canola oil

1 lb. lean beef, cut into 1-inch pieces

1 cooking apple, peeled, cored, shredded

1 carrot, shredded

½ yellow onion, peeled and sliced

1 clove garlic, minced

12 oz. can beer

½ c. beef broth

2 t. Worcestershire sauce

¼ t. dried thyme

salt and pepper to taste

1 t. cornstarch

4 c. egg noodles, cooked al dente, drained and kept hot

¼ t. poppy seeds

In a large Dutch oven, heat the oil on medium. Add the meat and cook until the meat is browned on all sides. Add the apple, carrot, onion, garlic, beer, broth, ½ cup water and remaining seasonings. Stir well, cover, reduce the heat to low, and simmer for 2 hours, or until the beef is very tender. Combine the cornstarch with 1 tablespoon cold water until smooth. Add to the beef mixture and re-heat, stirring constantly, until the mixture thickens. Toss the poppy seeds with the noodles. Spoon the beef over the noodles to serve.

Pork Chili Verde

1 T. vegetable oil

1 lb. boneless pork loin, cut into small pieces

2 4 oz. cans green chilies, chopped

4 roma tomatoes, cored, seeded and chopped

¼ c. purple onion, chopped

¼ c. fresh cilantro, chopped

2 T. lime juice

¼ t. liquid hot sauce + more to taste

15 oz. can black beans with liquid

Heat the oil in a deep saucepan and add the pork loin pieces. Sauté over medium-high heat for 2 minutes, turning meat as it browns. Reduce the heat to low and add the green chilies, tomatoes, onion, cilantro, lime juice, hot sauce and black beans. Mix well to combine. Cover and simmer on low heat for 2½ to 3 hours.

Flaky Crust Turkey Pot Pie

SERVES 4

Using purchased phyllo pastry gives you the time-saving edge to create a delicious home-cooked meal in minutes! Toss salad greens with balsamic vinaigrette while the pie is baking and dinner is done.

1½-2 c. cooked turkey, cubed

2 c. frozen mixed vegetables, thawed

10¾ oz. can cream of mushroom soup (regular or lowfat)

¼ c. whole milk

salt and pepper to taste

1 pkg. phyllo pastry sheets, thawed

½ c. butter or margarine, melted

Preheat the oven to 400°F. Coat a 2-quart baking dish with cooking spray. Combine the turkey, vegetables, cream of mushroom soup, milk, salt and pepper in a large bowl and mix well. Spoon the mixture into the baking dish. Brush butter over 1 pastry sheet and place on the pie. Trim the edges to 1-inch beyond the pan size and secure edges with a bit of water. Repeat with 10 sheets of phyllo pastry and butter. Cut a small slit in through the layers of pastry and bake, uncovered, for 30-40 minutes, or until golden and cooked through.

Angelo's Spaghetti & Meatball Soup

SERVES 4

Easy prep and easy clean up make this soup the perfect weeknight meal.
Serve with crusty French bread and salad.

¾ lb. lean ground beef

½ c. Italian-seasoned bread crumbs

1 large onion, chopped, divided

1 clove garlic, minced

½ t. dried Italian seasoning

4 c. chicken broth

24 oz. jar prepared marinara sauce with mushrooms

salt and pepper to taste

4 oz. dry spaghetti noodles, broken in 2-inch pieces

8 oz. frozen Italian-style green beans, thawed

Parmesan cheese for garnish (optional)

Make the meatballs: combine the beef, bread crumbs, 1 tablespoon onion, garlic and Italian seasoning. Mix lightly and form into 24 meatballs. Refrigerate for 30 minutes.

In a large stockpot, combine the chicken broth, remaining onion, marinara sauce and salt and pepper to taste. Add the meatballs, cover and cook on medium-low heat for 50-60 minutes, or until the meatballs are cooked through. Add the noodles and beans and cook for 12 minutes on medium heat until the noodles are tender. Garnish each serving with grated Parmesan, if desired.

Split Pea Soup with Seasoned Croutons

SERVES 4 TO 6

Split peas are an excellent source of protein and fiber for a very low cost. Added to smoky ham and vegetables, the peas really shine through in this comforting soup.

1 lb. dried green split peas

8 c. water

1 bay leaf

2 onions, chopped

1 t. dried Italian seasoning

4 ribs celery, sliced

2 c. carrots, peeled, chopped

salt and pepper to taste

8 oz smoked ham, diced

1 c. seasoned croutons

Sort the peas and discard any debris. Place the peas, water and bay leaf in a large stockpot and heat to a boil. Remove any foam and reduce the heat to a simmer. Add the onions, cover, and simmer for 1 hour. Add the Italian seasoning, celery, carrots, salt and pepper to taste ; simmer for 30-45 minutes, or until the peas are very tender. Remove the bay leaf. Pureé one-half of the soup in a blender. Return it to the stockpot and add the ham. Stir, re-heat briefly before serving. Garnish each serving with croutons.

One Dish Meals

Chili & Cornbread Bake

SERVES 6 TO 8

One Dish Meals

This easy, one-dish meal is about as kid-friendly as it can be.
Chili and cornbread...all in one pan!

½ lb. lean ground beef

1 small onion, peeled, chopped

1 clove garlic, minced

15 oz. can chili beans, reserve
¼ cup liquid

11 oz. can Mexican corn,
drained

2 T. ground chili powder

½ t. black pepper

1 T. all-purpose flour

1 c. dry baking mix

½ c. canned creamed corn

½ c. yellow cornmeal

1 large egg, beaten

1 T. sugar

1 c. lowfat milk

Preheat the oven to 350⁰F. Lightly coat a 9 x 13-inch baking pan with cooking spray. Brown the beef in a skillet and drain excess fat. Add the onion and garlic and sauté for 2 minutes on medium heat. Add the beans, corn, chili powder and black pepper and mix well. Mix together the reserved bean liquid and flour and add to the chili mixture. Heat to boiling and cook on medium until thickened. Spread the beef and beans in prepared pan. In a bowl, combine the baking mix, corn, cornmeal, egg, sugar and milk. Beat to form a soft batter. Turn the batter over the chili mix and spread evenly in the pan. Bake at 350ºF for 55-60 minutes, or until the cornbread and chili are cooked through and bubbly.

Country Shepherd's Pie

SERVES 4 TO 6

1 T. extra virgin olive oil

1 small white onion, chopped

1 clove garlic, minced

½ lb. lean ground beef

½ c. celery, chopped

1 c. carrots, peeled, chopped

1 t. dried Italian seasoning

salt and pepper to taste

1 c. vegetable broth

2 pkgs instant mashed potatoes + water as directed

1 T. butter

¼ c. mild cheddar cheese, shredded

Preheat the oven to 350ºF. Sauté the onion and garlic in the oil in an oven-proof roasting pan until soft. Add the beef and sauté until cooked through. Drain excess grease. Add the celery, carrots, seasonings and broth, cover and bake for 30 minutes, or until the vegetables are soft. Prepare the mashed potatoes, add butter and cheese and blend well. Spread the potatoes evenly over the meat and vegetables. Bake, uncovered, for 10 minutes, until potatoes are golden.

One Dish Meals

21

Toasted Almond Turkey Bowls

SERVES 4

3 T. butter

¼ c. all-purpose flour

2 c. whole or lowfat milk

3 T. dry white wine

salt and pepper to taste

¼ t. garlic salt

2 c. cooked turkey meat, diced

1 c. frozen peas, thawed

2 T. almonds, slivered, toasted

3 c. brown rice, cooked, kept warm

¼ c. Parmesan cheese, grated

In a saucepan over low heat, melt the butter. Add the flour and stir until smooth. Cook 1 minute, stirring constantly. Gradually add the milk, and stir over low heat until thickened. Add the wine and seasonings and blend. Simmer for 2 minutes. Add the turkey, peas and almonds and warm through. To serve, place rice in 4 individual bowls, and cover with turkey and sauce. Garnish with cheese before serving.

Make-Ahead Ham & Potato Bake

SERVES 8

1 c. cooked ham, cut into small cubes

4 c. frozen hash browned potatoes

1 green pepper, diced

½ c. onion, chopped

1 c. mild cheddar cheese, shredded

3 c. whole or lowfat milk

1 c. dry baking mix

salt and pepper to taste

4 large eggs

Coat a 9 x 13-inch baking pan with cooking spray. Spread the ham and potatoes over the bottom of the pan. Layer the green pepper, onion and cheddar cheese on top of the potatoes. Mix together in a large bowl the milk, baking mix, salt, pepper and eggs and beat well. Pour over the ham and vegetables. Cover tightly and refrigerate for 4-12 hours. To serve, unwrap and bake at 375°F for 30-40 minutes or until bubbly and heated through.

Santa Fe Tamale Pie

SERVES 4 TO 6

2 T. vegetable oil

1 c. yellow onion, chopped

1 c. canned whole kernel corn

1 c. canned diced tomatoes

1 c. ripe olives, sliced

3 cloves garlic, minced

½ t. salt

3 T. ground chili powder

3 eggs, beaten

1¼ c. milk

2 c. yellow cornmeal

1 t. baking powder

Chili Pepper Sauce:

8 oz. can tomato sauce

8 oz. water

1 T. green pepper, chopped

1 T. cornstarch

1 T. ground chili powder

½ t. salt

Preheat the oven to 350ºF. Heat the oil in a sauté pan and add the onion, corn, tomatoes, olives and garlic. Sauté for 4-6 minutes. In a medium bowl, blend the salt, chili powder, eggs, milk, cornmeal and baking powder until smooth. Coat an 8 x 10-inch baking pan with cooking spray and add the vegetables. Spoon the cornmeal mixture over the vegetables and gently stir. Bake for 30-40 minutes until firm.

Prepare the Chili Pepper Sauce by combining the tomato sauce, water, green pepper, cornstarch, ground chili powder and salt in a small saucepan. Heat and stir until boiling. Reduce the heat and simmer for 5 minutes. Serve the tamale pie with the sauce on the side.

One Dish Meals

Inside-Out Enchiladas

1 lb. lean ground beef

10 corn tortillas, torn into small pieces

15 oz. can refried beans

10 oz. can enchilada sauce

1 c. cheddar cheese, shredded

2 c. iceberg lettuce, shredded

¼ c. green onions, chopped

2 tomatoes, chopped

Preheat the oven to 375^{0}F. Brown the beef in a 3-quart baking dish. Drain excess grease and set beef aside. Layer the tortilla pieces over the bottom of the dish, smooth the beans over evenly, and cover with the beef. Top with the enchilada sauce and cheese. Bake, uncovered, for 20-25 minutes, until hot. Top each serving with lettuce, onions and tomato. Serves 4.

Turkey Taco Tortilla Stack

SERVES 4 TO 6

1 lb. ground turkey

1 T. dry taco seasoning

1 medium onion, chopped

1 c. fresh salsa (or use 8 oz. jar), divided

½ c. sour cream

10¾ oz. can cream of mushroom soup

6 corn tortillas, cut into strips

½ c. cheddar cheese, shredded

sliced black olives for garnish

Preheat the oven to 350^{0}F. Sauté the turkey, seasoning and onion in a sauté pan. Spread ½ cup of salsa on the bottom of an 8 x 8-inch baking dish. Mix the remaining salsa, sour cream and soup.

Place half of the tortilla strips on top of the salsa in the dish. Layer with half of the cooked turkey mixture. Layer half of the soup mixture and finally layer half of the cheese. Repeat the layers once. Bake uncovered for 30-40 minutes or until bubbly. Garnish with olives, if desired.

Skillet Steak & Potatoes

SERVES 4

1 lb. round steak, cut into 4 individual portions

½ c. flour

salt and pepper to taste

1 T. canola or vegetable oil

1 c. beef broth

1 c. tomato vegetable juice

½ white onion, sliced

1 green bell pepper, sliced

3 russet potatoes, peeled, cut in chunks

Dredge the beef in the flour, salt and pepper to taste. Heat the oil in a large Dutch oven or stockpot until hot and add the beef. Brown each piece and remove. Add flour over the browned bits in the bottom of the pan. Stir and add the broth and juice; cook for 1 minute on medium. Add the onion, pepper, potatoes and beef. Cover tightly and simmer for 2 hours, or until the steak is very tender and the vegetables are cooked.

Southwestern Chicken & Summer Vegetables

SERVES 4

Serve over crispy tortilla chips or spoon into flour tortillas.

6 oz. pkg herb-flavored crumb coating mix

2 large boneless, skinless chicken breasts

3 c. zucchini, scrubbed and thinly sliced

1 small white onion, thinly sliced

1 red pepper, sliced

1 c. prepared salsa

Preheat the oven to 400°F. Cut each chicken breast in half horizontally to create thin fillets. Dredge the chicken in the coating mixture. Place the chicken in a 9 x 13-inch roasting pan and surround with the zucchini, onion and peppers. Spoon the salsa over all. Bake, covered, for 30 minutes, or until the chicken is cooked through.

Weeknight Chili Beef Skillet

One Dish Meals

1 lb. lean ground beef

1 white onion, chopped

8 oz. tomato sauce

1 c. beef broth

½ t. dried oregano

½ t. dried thyme

1 T. fresh parsley, minced

2 t. chili seasoning

15 oz. can whole kernel corn, drained

8 oz. pkg. broad egg noodles, cooked and drained

¼ c. Parmesan cheese, grated

Sauté the beef in a skillet and crumble with a fork. Drain grease and add the onion. Sauté for 2 minutes. Add the tomato sauce, broth, oregano, thyme, parsley and chili seasoning and mix well. Add the corn and noodles and mix all ingredients together. Cover and simmer on medium heat until hot, about 7 minutes. Garnish with cheese before serving.

New England Clam Chowder in Sourdough Bowls

SERVES 4

1 T. vegetable oil

2 T. onion, chopped

4 T. butter

4 T. flour

1½ t. salt

½ t. freshly ground black pepper

4 c. whole or lowfat milk

6½ oz. can clams, chopped

2 small russet potatoes, peeled, cubed

4 individual sourdough bread rounds

2 T. fresh parsley, chopped (optional)

Heat the oil on medium heat in a stockpot and add the onion. Sauté until soft and add the butter. Add the flour and stir constantly for 2 minutes. Add the salt and pepper and continue stirring as the mixture thickens. Slowly add the milk with a whisk, blending well. Bring to a boil, reduce the heat to simmer and add the clams and potatoes. Adjust seasonings and simmer for 20 minutes. Remove the inner part of each bread round, leaving a 1-inch crust in each bowl. Serve the soup in the bread bowls; garnish with parsley, if using.

Crab & Cheese Melts

SERVES 4

Although crab meat can be expensive, it is economical when combined with other delicious ingredients. Served hot in a crab melt over crispy bread, it is exquisite.

Super Easy 3-Step Meals

6-8 oz. canned crab meat, shredded

2 T. butter, softened

½ c. lowfat mayonnaise

1 clove garlic, minced

3 T. fresh parsley, chopped

1 t. ground paprika

1 large French baguette, split horizontally, quartered, toasted

4 slices American cheese singles, each cut into 2 triangles

Step 1: Mix together the crab, butter, mayonnaise, garlic, parsley and paprika in a bowl.

Step 2: Cover the bread with the crab mixture.

Step 3: Broil the sandwiches until the crab is bubbly. Add the cheese slices and broil until melted.

3-Step Ham & Lima Bean Soup

SERVES 6 TO 8

Bean soup deserves a smoky, rich ham hock to bring out the best flavor. This soup takes time to prepare, but it is very easy and the ham and beans provide a great source of protein.

1 ham hock with meat

6 c. water

4 yellow onions, peeled, roughly cut

3 cloves garlic, minced

5 ribs celery, chopped

2 15 oz. cans lima beans, drained

1 t. ground black pepper

28 oz. can diced tomatoes with juices

salt to taste

Step 1: Cook the ham hock in a stockpot with the water, onions, garlic and celery on medium-low for 1 hour.

Step 2: Remove the ham hock and remove the meat from the bone. Discard the hock and return the meat to the soup.

Step 3: Add the remaining ingredients, adjust seasonings to taste, simmer for 15 minutes and serve.

Rustic Chicken, Tomato & Black Bean Salad

SERVES 4

1 c. cooked chicken, shredded

1 c. canned black beans, rinsed and drained

1 c. ripe tomatoes, diced

½ c. red onion, diced

½ c. green bell pepper, diced

½ c. canned corn kernels

2 T. extra virgin olive oil

1 t. cider vinegar

1 t. ground cumin

salt and pepper to taste

Step 1: Toss together the chicken, beans, tomatoes, onion, bell pepper and corn in a serving bowl.

Step 2: In a small bowl, whisk together the oil, vinegar, cumin, salt and pepper.

Step 3: Drizzle the dressing over the salad and toss to coat. Serve at once or chill before serving.

Turkey, Walnut & Melon Salad with Creamy Dressing

SERVES 4

½ large cantaloupe, cubed

2 c. cooked turkey, chopped (use cooked chicken, if desired)

½ c. celery, chopped

¼ c. walnuts, chopped

1 green onion, thinly sliced

Creamy Dressing:

3 oz. cream cheese, softened

1 T. lowfat milk

¼ t. ground cinnamon

Step 1: Place the cantaloupe, turkey, celery, walnuts and green onion in a serving bowl.

Step 2: In a small bowl, combine the cream cheese, milk and cinnamon; whisk until smooth.

Step 3: Pour the dressing over the salad and toss lightly. Serve right away or chill before serving.

Chicken & Cheese Stuffed Peppers

SERVES 4 TO 6

3 red peppers, cored, cut in half horizontally

7 oz. pkg rice pilaf mix, prepared

1 c. cooked chicken, chopped

½ t. ground marjoram

salt and pepper to taste

1 small zucchini, chopped

¼ c. Parmesan cheese, grated

½ c. mozzarella cheese, shredded

Step 1: Preheat the oven to 350°F. Coat a 9 x 13-inch baking dish with cooking spray. Combine the rice, chicken, seasonings, zucchini and Parmesan cheese in a large bowl.

Step 2: Fill each half pepper with the chicken mix, mounding slightly. Place the stuffed peppers in the prepared pan. Sprinkle with the mozzarella cheese.

Step 3: Bake, uncovered, for 20 minutes or until hot throughout.

Baked Chicken & Broccoli

SERVES 4

Super Easy 3-Step Meals

5 oz. chicken pilaf rice mix

4 chicken breast halves

1 large onion, cut into wedges

2 c. fresh broccoli, chopped (or use frozen, thawed broccoli)

2½ c. chicken broth

2 T. extra virgin olive oil

1 T. rice wine vinegar

1 T. garlic, minced

salt and pepper to taste

Step 1: Preheat the oven to 375°F. Coat a large baking pan with cooking spray. Place the rice mix in the bottom of the pan. Layer the chicken, onion and the broccoli over the rice.

Step 2: Mix together the broth, oil, vinegar, garlic, salt and pepper and pour over all.

Step 3: Cover tightly and bake for 1 hour, or until the chicken is cooked completely through.

Stove Top Pork Chops in Tomato Pepper Sauce

SERVES 4

1 T. extra virgin olive oil

4 pork loin chops, 1-inch thick

1 c. long grain white rice, uncooked

1 large onion, peeled, sliced

3 large, ripe tomatoes, sliced

1 green bell pepper, sliced

2 c. beef broth

¼ t. dried marjoram

¼ t. dried thyme

salt and pepper to taste

Step 1: Heat the oil in a large skillet and sear the pork on both sides. Spread the rice around the chops.

Step 2: Over medium heat, layer the vegetables over the rice. Combine the broth with the seasonings and pour over all. Heat on medium-high until broth comes to a boil.

Step 3: Cover tightly and reduce heat to medium-low for 30-40 minutes, or until pork is cooked through.

Irish Supper Soup

SERVES 4

½ lb. cooked ham, chopped

1 T. vegetable oil

3 russet potatoes, peeled, cubed

1 large onion, thinly sliced

1 carrot, peeled, chopped

5 c. beef broth

1 c. water

salt and pepper to taste

½ head green cabbage, shredded

Step 1: Place the ham in a stockpot and add the oil. Sauté for 2 minutes, stirring often.

Step 2: Add the remaining ingredients, except the cabbage, and simmer for 45 minutes, covered.

Step 3: Add the cabbage and simmer for 10 minutes.

Chicken, Spinach & Mandarin Salad

SERVES 4

Tangy Mustard Dressing:

¼ c. extra virgin olive oil

2 T. cider vinegar

2 T. sugar

½ t. salt

¼ t. ground black pepper

¼ t. dry mustard

½ t. celery seed

Salad:

1½ lbs. fresh spinach, rinsed and torn

¼ c. red onion, chopped

11 oz. can mandarin orange slices, drained

1½ c. cooked chicken, cubed

1 c. celery, chopped

¼ c. walnuts, chopped

Step 1: In a small bowl, whisk together the olive oil, vinegar, sugar, salt, pepper, mustard and celery seed. Chill for 30 minutes or up to 12 hours.

Step 2: In a serving bowl, toss together the remaining ingredients.

Step 3: Drizzle the dressing over the salad and toss to coat.

Greek Chicken with Baby Reds & Tomatoes

SERVES 4

5 oz. pkg wild rice mix, uncooked

2 zucchini, sliced

1 lb. baby red potatoes, cut in half

2 cloves garlic, minced

2 c. tomatoes, diced

1 t. dried Italian seasoning

2 T. lemon juice

salt and pepper to taste

2 boneless chicken breasts, cut in half horizontally

3½ c. chicken broth

Step 1: Preheat the oven to 375°F. Coat a large roasting pan with cooking spray.

Step 2: Spread the rice mix on the bottom of the pan. Layer the vegetables, seasonings, and chicken over the rice. Pour the chicken broth over all.

Step 3: Bake, covered, for 45-55 minutes until the chicken is cooked through completely.

Super Easy 3-Step Meals

Pan de la Hote

SERVES 4 TO 6

This meatless Mexican entrée is filled with subtly rich cheese and chilies. Serve with cold vegetables for a complete and easy meal.

1 c. dry baking mix

1 egg, beaten

1 T. sugar

17 oz. can creamed corn

½ c. dairy sour cream

1 lb. Jack cheese, sliced

7 oz. can whole green chilies

Step 1: Preheat the oven to 350°F. Combine the baking mix, egg, sugar, creamed corn and sour cream. Mix well and spread half of the mixture into a greased 2-quart baking pan.

Step 2: Cover with half of the cheese slices. Top with half of the chilies. Repeat the layers.

Step 3: Bake for 20-35 minutes until lightly browned and cooked through.

Antipasto Salami Salad

SERVES 4 TO 6

2 c. small pasta shells, cooked and drained

1 red pepper, chopped

½ c. ripe olives, sliced

1 small purple onion, chopped

½ c. mozzarella cheese, cut into small cubes

3 oz. salami, cut into thin strips

2 T. dry Italian salad dressing mix

2 T. extra virgin olive oil

2 T. water

Step 1: In a large serving bowl, combine the pasta, red peppers, olives, onion, cheese and salami.

Step 2: Mix together the Italian salad dressing mix, olive oil and water drizzle over the salad. Toss well.

Step 3: Cover and refrigerate for 1 hour or up to overnight before serving.

Creamy Ham & Scalloped Potatoes

SERVES 6 TO 8

3 large baking potatoes, peeled, thinly sliced

½ lb. cooked ham, chopped

½ c. Romano cheese, shredded

1½ c. half and half cream

salt and pepper to taste

Step 1: Preheat the oven to 350°F. Coat a 9 x 13-inch baking pan with cooking spray. Arrange the potatoes in the pan.

Step 2: Stir the ham and cheese into the cream and pour over the potatoes. Adjust the seasonings to taste.

Step 3: Cover and bake for 1 hour, until the potatoes are tender.

Chuckwagon Tomato Bean Chili

Super Easy 3-Step Meals

2 oz. small pasta shells (about ⅔ cup)

1 c. prepared mild salsa

¾ c. water

1 T. ground extra-spicy chili powder

15 oz. can kidney beans, drained

8 oz. can tomato sauce

½ c. American cheese, shredded

fresh parsley for garnish

Step 1: Combine the pasta shells, salsa, water and chili powder in a large skillet. Mix and heat on medium heat to boiling.

Step 2: Reduce the heat to simmer and add the beans and tomato sauce. Cover and simmer for 15-20 minutes, or until the pasta is tender.

Step 3: Garnish with cheese and parsley and serve in bowls.

Crispy Parmesan Chicken Dinner

SERVES 4

3 T. canola oil

1 egg, beaten

1 c. all-purpose flour

1 t. black pepper

½ c. Parmesan cheese, grated

3 boneless, skinless chicken breasts, cut into 1-inch strips

6 Yukon gold potatoes, quartered

salt and pepper to taste

Step 1: Preheat the oven to 400°F. Pour the oil into a 9 x 13-inch roasting pan.

Step 2: Place the egg in a shallow dish and mix the flour, pepper and cheese in a plastic bag.

Step 3: Dip each chicken strip in the egg and then in the flour/cheese mix, pressing crumbs to adhere to the chicken. Arrange the chicken strips and potatoes in the pan. Bake, uncovered, for 1 hour, or until chicken is cooked through completely.

Mandarin Chicken Salad

SERVES 4

2 heads romaine lettuce, washed and torn into small pieces

11 oz. can mandarin oranges, liquid reserved

¼ c. blanched almonds, chopped

½ small purple onion, sliced into thin rings

freshly grated black pepper

2 c. cooked chicken breast, chopped

Orange Honey Dressing:

¼ c. mandarin orange juice (juice from can plus water)

2 T. honey

¼ c. sesame oil

3 T. raspberry vinegar

Step 1: Mix together the lettuce, oranges, almonds and onions in a large bowl.

Step 2: In a small bowl, combine the orange juice, honey, oil and vinegar. Whisk and pour over the salad.

Step 3: Divide the salad among 4 plates and top each with chicken. Drizzle the dressing over each salad.

Almost Instant Taco Salad

SERVES 4

¾ lb. lean ground beef

2 T. dry taco seasoning mix

2 heads romaine lettuce, chopped

1 c. Monterey Jack cheese, shredded

1 c. canned black beans, drained

1 ripe tomato, cut into small chunks

½ small white onion, chopped

½ c. prepared salsa

2 c. tortilla chips, slightly crushed

Step 1: Brown the beef in a large skillet and drain; mix in seasoning mixture and combine.

Step 2: Arrange the lettuce on 4 plates and layer each with cheese. Cover the cheese with the beef.

Step 3: Top each salad with black beans, tomato, onion and salsa. Cover with the chips before serving.

Ham & Cheese Pockets

SERVES 4

4 sheets phyllo pastry dough

4 T. butter, melted

1 c. cooked ham, finely chopped

1 c. sharp cheddar cheese, shredded

1 large tart apple, chopped

1 clove garlic, minced

¼ c. buttery cracker crumbs

Preheat the oven to 350°F. Place 1 sheet pastry on a lightly-floured board. Brush with butter and repeat with remaining pastry sheets and butter. Cut the stack into 4 squares and arrange on a baking sheet. Combine the ham, cheese, apple, garlic and crumbs. Divide the filling onto 4 pastry squares. Bake for 15-20 minutes, or until golden brown.

Fresh Vegetable & Cheese Wraps

SERVES 4

1 small zucchini, chopped

1 medium carrot, peeled, chopped

1 cucumber, peeled, finely chopped

1 green pepper, diced

2 green onions, chopped

2 cloves garlic, crushed

½ c. cream cheese, softened

2 t. ground chili powder

½ ripe avocado, mashed

4 8-inch flour tortillas

Combine the chopped vegetables in a bowl. Blend the garlic, cheese, chili powder and avocado in a separate bowl. Place 1 tortilla on a flat surface. Thinly spread the cream cheese mixture on the tortilla. Spoon one-fourth of the vegetables over the cheese and roll the tortilla tightly, tucking in the ends. Repeat with the remaining tortillas and filling. Chill for 15 minutes before serving.

Turkey & Cranberries with Ancient Grains

SERVES 4

¼ c. butter

1 small white onion, peeled, diced

1 clove garlic, minced

½ c. celery, minced

4 c. chicken broth

2 c. bulgur wheat, uncooked

1 t. salt

¼ c. dried cranberries

2 c. cooked turkey, shredded

½ c. fresh parsley, chopped

In a large saucepan over medium-high heat, sauté the onion, garlic and celery in the butter until tender, about 5 minutes. Add the chicken broth, bulgur and salt. Bring to a boil. Cover, reduce heat to low and simmer for 15-20 minutes until bulgur is tender. Drain excess liquid and add the cranberries, turkey and parsley, mixing lightly. Heat 5 minutes before serving.

Hot Pepper Sauce Shrimp Skillet

¼ c. butter

1 medium yellow onion, chopped

4 cloves garlic, chopped

1 t. celery salt

1 t. dry mustard

¼ t. ground cloves

¼ t. ground ginger

¼ t. ground paprika

½ t. ground black pepper

2 t. hot pepper sauce

2 t. fresh lemon juice

1½ lbs. medium-size fresh shrimp, deveined, peeled

3 c. cooked long grain white rice, kept warm

4 slices bacon, cooked, crumbled

In a large skillet, melt the butter and add the onion, garlic, seasonings and hot pepper sauce. Stir and sauté until the onion is tender, about 5 minutes. Stir in the lemon juice and shrimp. Sauté for 5 to 7 minutes, or until the shrimp turns completely pink. Arrange the rice on a serving platter, cover with the shrimp and sauce, and garnish with the bacon.

Chicken Scaloppini with Angel Hair Pasta

SERVES 4

2 boneless chicken breasts, cut in half horizontally

1 T. canola oil

1 purple onion, thinly sliced

1 clove garlic, minced

3 mushrooms, thinly sliced

1 zucchini, thinly sliced

15 oz. can Italian-style stewed tomatoes

salt and pepper to taste

1 t. dried Italian seasoning

8 oz. angel hair pasta, cooked

grated Parmesan cheese for garnish (optional)

Heat the oil in a skillet and sauté the chicken until cooked through, 4-5 minutes. Cover and keep warm.

Place the vegetables and seasonings in the skillet and sauté for 8-10 minutes on medium heat, stirring often. Return the chicken to the skillet and cook with the vegetables for 2 minutes. Serve over the cooked pasta. Garnish with cheese, if desired.

30-Minute Meals

Pepper Jack Chicken Enchiladas

SERVES 4 TO 6

4 T. butter or margarine

4 T. flour

8 oz. can tomato sauce

3 c. water

2 T. extra spicy ground chili powder

1 t. salt

10 6-inch corn tortillas, warmed

2 c. cooked chicken, shredded

1 c. Pepper Jack cheese, shredded

Coat a 9 x 13-inch baking pan with cooking spray. Preheat the oven to 350°F. In a medium saucepan, melt the butter on low heat and add the flour. Stir and cook until thick and smooth. Add the tomato sauce, water, chili powder and salt, whisking to blend well. Bring to a boil then reduce the heat to medium. Fill each tortilla with the chicken and cheese, roll and place in the pan. Cover with the sauce and top with remaining cheese. Bake for 30 minutes, until bubbly and hot.

Beef Mushroom Stroganoff

SERVES 4 TO 6

2 T. canola oil

1 c. onions, chopped

¾ lb. strip or hangar steak, sliced thinly across the grain

1 t. black pepper (+ more to taste)

10¾ oz. can cream of mushroom soup

¼ c. half and half cream

1 c. sour cream

1 lb. wide egg noodles, cooked

Chopped parsley for garnish (optional)

Heat the oil in a skillet and add the onions; sauté for 2 minutes. Reduce the heat to medium and add the beef. Season with pepper and sauté for 3 minutes. Keep warm. Combine the soup, cream and sour cream. Add the sauce to the beef on low heat, stirring to combine. Adjust seasonings and simmer for 3-4 minutes. Serve beef and sauce over noodles and garnish with parsley, if using.

Sweet & Sour Pork with Jasmine Rice

SERVES 4

2 T. canola oil

2 cloves garlic, minced

3 carrots, peeled and sliced

1 onion, peeled, roughly cut

1 lb. boneless pork, cut into
1-inch pieces

1 green pepper, roughly cut

15¼ oz. can pineapple chunks,
with juice reserved

2 T. rice wine vinegar

1 t. ground ginger

2 T. soy sauce

2 T. cornstarch

2 T. water

4 c. hot, cooked
Jasmine rice

Heat the oil in a skillet; add the garlic, carrots, onion, and pork and cook over medium heat for 4-5 minutes. Add the green pepper and pineapple and cook for 2 minutes. Blend together the reserved juice, vinegar, ginger and soy sauce. Add to the pork and vegetables. Combine the cornstarch and water and pour over the pork mixture; heat to a boil and stir until thickened. Serve over the rice.

Greek Lamb with Lemon & Feta Cheese

Lamb is expensive, however it complements pasta and fresh lemon beautifully. One-half pound goes a long way in this delicious recipe.

½ lb. ground lamb

½ c. onion, chopped

1 clove garlic, minced

15 oz. can beef broth

1½ c. penne pasta, uncooked

15 oz. can diced tomatoes, with juices

2 c. frozen cut green beans, thawed

¼ c. tomato sauce

½ t. ground oregano

¼ t. ground cinnamon

crumbled feta cheese for garnish

Sauté the lamb in a skillet; add the onion and garlic and cook for 3 minutes. Drain excess fat. Add the broth and bring to a boil. Add the pasta and simmer, covered, for 7 minutes. Add the remaining ingredients, except cheese, and cook on low until the vegetables are tender. Garnish with feta cheese just before serving.

30-Minute Meals

49

Italian Sausage Pasta Bowls

1 lb. mild or spicy sausage, casings removed

2 cloves garlic, chopped

1 large onion, chopped

1 green pepper, chopped

2 c. crushed Italian-style tomatoes

1 t. salt

½ t. freshly ground black pepper

1 lb. rigatoni pasta, cooked

¼ lb. mozzarella cheese, shredded

Sauté the sausage in a skillet until cooked, crumbling the meat with a fork. Add the garlic and onion and continue cooking for 2 minutes. Add the vegetables and seasonings and cook for 10 minutes. Remove from the heat and toss with the pasta. Top with the cheese before serving.

Pork & Vegetable Chow Mein

SERVES 4 TO 6

1 lb. lean pork, thinly sliced

¼ c. cornstarch, divided

1 t. sugar

⅓ c. soy sauce

2 T. sesame oil

2 c. water, divided

2 c. celery, sliced

1 large onion, sliced

1 clove garlic, minced

2 c. fresh broccoli, cut in small florets

4 oz. can water chestnuts, sliced

4 oz. jar mushrooms, drained

1 red pepper, thinly sliced

2 green onions, thinly sliced

crispy Chinese noodles

Marinate the pork for 10 minutes with 2 tablespoons cornstarch, sugar, and 1 tablespoon of soy sauce. Heat the oil in a skillet on medium high and add the pork, remaining soy sauce and 1½ cups water. Simmer on low for 8 minutes. Add the vegetables and simmer for 5 minutes. Blend the remaining cornstarch with ½ cup of water and add to the chow mein. Cook and stir over medium heat until the sauce is smooth. Serve over the crispy noodles.

Pork Chops Marrakech

SERVES 4

4 center cut pork chops, ½-inch thick (or use boneless loin chops)

2 T. extra virgin olive oil, divided

1 clove garlic, minced

¼ c. white onion, chopped

½ c. carrots, finely chopped

½ c. celery, finely chopped

5½ oz. garlic and mushroom couscous mix

1½ c. chicken broth

2 green onions, thinly sliced

Heat 1 tablespoon oil in a skillet and add the pork; sear on medium-high heat for 2 minutes per side. Remove and keep warm. Add 1 tablespoon oil to the pan, reduce the heat to medium and add the garlic, onion, carrots and celery. Cook for 3-4 minutes, stirring well. Add the couscous and the seasoning packet, the chicken broth and green onions and bring to a boil. Reduce the heat to simmer, add the pork chops, cover and cook for 7-9 minutes, or until the chops are cooked through and the couscous is tender.

Sour Cream Beef with Crimini Mushrooms

SERVES 4

1 lb. beef steak, sliced thinly

¼ c. unsalted butter

2 c. crimini mushrooms, sliced

1 small white onion, chopped

¼ c. beef broth

1 c. sour cream

salt and pepper to taste

4 c. hot, cooked rice

Sauté the beef in the butter in a skillet for 2 minutes, turning the slices occasionally. Add the mushrooms and onion and cook on low for 2 minutes. Add the broth and heat through, stirring slow to blend. Slowly add the sour cream, stirring well to blend. Add the pepper and salt and stir again. Serve immediately over hot rice.

Salmon & Walnut Pesto Linguine

SERVES 4

1 lb. salmon fillets, cut into
1 x 3-inch slices

2 T. extra virgin olive oil

1 lb. linguine pasta, cooked and
drained

2 T. walnuts, finely minced

½ c. prepared pesto sauce

Parmesan cheese, grated,
for garnish

Sauté the salmon in the oil in a skillet for 2 minutes. Turn and sauté for 5 minutes. Set aside and keep warm. Place the pasta in a large serving bowl. Add the walnuts and pesto to the pasta and toss. Add the salmon and toss lightly again. Garnish with Parmesan cheese before.

Chicken & Zucchini Ziti

SERVES 4

2 T. extra virgin olive oil

1 lb. chicken breast, cubed

3 c. dry ziti pasta, uncooked

2 zucchini, sliced thinly

32 oz. jar prepared spaghetti
sauce with mushrooms
and onion

1 c. water

1 c. mozzarella cheese,
shredded

Heat the oil in a large skillet and add the chicken. Sauté, turning the chicken as it cooks until no pink remains. Add the pasta, zucchini, spaghetti sauce and water and mix well. Cover with the cheese and reduce the heat to simmer. Cover and continue cooking on medium-low for 20-25 minutes, until the pasta is tender.

Stuffed & Double-Stuffed Chicken

SERVES 4

2 c. seasoned herb bread stuffing

2 T. butter

½ c. water, heated to boiling

1 T. fresh parsley, minced

½ c. yellow onion, finely chopped

1 rib celery, finely chopped

4 boneless chicken breasts

2 c. chicken broth

½ c. Parmesan cheese, grated

Preheat the oven to 375°F. Combine the stuffing mix, butter and hot water. Toss and add the parsley, onion and celery. Cut a slit sideways in each chicken breast to form a pocket and pack each breast with stuffing. Coat a 9 x 13-inch baking pan with cooking spray. Arrange the chicken and remaining stuffing mix in the pan and pour the broth over all. Spoon the cheese on top and cover. Bake for 45 minutes, or until the chicken is cooked completely through.

Saucy Spanish Rice

SERVES 4 TO 6

2 c. quick-cooking rice

2 15 oz. cans diced tomatoes, with juices

1 green pepper, chopped

1 small white onion, chopped

1 t. ground chili powder

1 t. salt

1 t. black pepper

1 lb. spicy sausage, cooked and crumbled

Preheat the oven to 350°F. Coat a 2-quart casserole dish with cooking spray. Spoon the rice, tomatoes, green pepper, onion, chili powder, salt and pepper into the pan and mix lightly. Scatter the sausage over all and bake for 20-25 minutes, until the rice is tender.

Glazed Pork Chops & Potatoes

SERVES 4

4 boneless pork chops

12 oz. dark beer

¼ c. honey mustard

2 cloves garlic, minced

4 oz. instant mashed potatoes, prepared

Place the chops on a broiler pan and set the oven to broil. In a small bowl, combine the beer, mustard and garlic. Brush over the chops several times as they broil, turning several times. When cooked through completely and no pink remains, slice and serve the pork over the mashed potatoes.

Classic Chicken Cacciatore

MAKES 4 SERVINGS

Meal Inspiration

1 c. flour

salt and pepper to taste

½ t. ground paprika

3-4 lb. roasting chicken, cut into pieces

3 T. canola oil

1 medium onion, chopped

3 cloves garlic, minced

4 oz. mushrooms, sliced

15 oz. can diced tomatoes, with juices

6 oz. can tomato paste

¼ c. Marsala wine (optional)

1 t. dried Italian seasoning

1 c. green beans (use canned or frozen, thawed beans)

1 lb. linguini noodles, cooked until tender

Parmesan cheese, grated, for garnish

In a large plastic bag, combine the flour, salt, pepper and paprika. Dredge the chicken pieces in the mixture. Heat the oil in a large stockpot until hot. Add the chicken and cook on medium-high heat for 6-7 minutes, turning the chicken as it browns. Remove the chicken and set aside. Sauté the onions and garlic in the pan drippings for 2-3 minutes and add the mushrooms, tomatoes and tomato paste. Stir and add the wine and Italian seasoning and mix again. Return the chicken to the pot, cover and simmer for 30-35 minutes, or until the chicken is completely cooked through. Add the green beans and heat for 5 minutes. Serve the chicken and sauce over the pasta and garnish with cheese.

Mediterranean-Spiced Chicken & Barley

SERVES 4 TO 6

1½ t. ground cumin

1½ t. ground chili powder

1 t. salt

1 t. ground cinnamon

1 t. dried mint flakes

1 t. garlic powder

1 t. ground red pepper (or use black pepper, if desired)

6 skinless chicken thighs

1 T. olive oil

1 large onion, chopped

2 T. soy sauce

1 T. sherry

3½ c. chicken broth

1¼ c. uncooked pearl barley

14.5 oz. can diced tomatoes, drained

chopped green onions, for garnish

Combine the spices in a bowl; rub one-half of mixture over chicken thighs. Heat oil in a skillet over medium-high heat and sauté the chicken on each side. Remove chicken. Place the remaining ingredients in the skillet, including the rest of the spice mixture, and blend. Add the chicken and bring to a boil on high heat. Reduce the heat, cover and simmer 45-55 minutes, until the chicken is cooked through. Garnish with the green onions.

Coq au Vin

SERVES 4

3 slices bacon, chopped

4 chicken thighs

1 yellow onion, chopped

salt and pepper to taste

2 c. baby carrots

1 c. mushrooms, sliced

2 c. chicken broth

1 c. red wine

1 T. fresh parsley, chopped

Preheat the oven to 375°F. Place the bacon in an oven-proof roasting pan and sauté on medium-high heat for 1 minute. Add the chicken thighs and brown thighs, turning once. Add the remaining ingredients, except the parsley, and stir lightly. Cover tightly and roast for 1½ hours, or until the chicken is completely cooked through. Garnish with parsley before serving.

Tomato, Bacon & Swiss Cheese Quiche

SERVES 4 TO 6

2 c. Swiss cheese, shredded

4 slices bacon, cooked and crumbled

1½ c. whole or lowfat milk

4 large eggs, beaten

2 T. green onions, chopped

salt and pepper to taste

1 9-inch refrigerated deep-dish pie crust

1 medium tomato, cut into ¼-inch thick slices

Preheat the oven to 400°F. In a large bowl, combine the cheese, bacon, milk, eggs, onions, and salt and pepper to taste. Mix well and spoon into the crust. Bake for 30 minutes. Arrange the tomatoes on top of the quiche and continue baking for 10-15 minutes, or until a knife inserted in the center comes out clean. Serve warm or cold.

Orzo Minestrone

2 T. extra-virgin olive oil

1 large onion, chopped

2 cloves garlic, minced

2 carrots, peeled, diced

2 ribs celery, chopped

1 c. green beans

15 oz. can diced tomatoes

1 c. tomato sauce

2 bay leaves

1 t. dried Italian seasoning

¾ c. orzo pasta

16 oz. can garbanzo beans, drained and rinsed

salt and pepper to taste

Parmesan cheese, grated, for garnish

Heat the oil in a large stockpot and add the onion and garlic; sauté until soft. Add the remaining ingredients, except the pasta and garbanzo beans. Simmer on low heat for 45 minutes. 15 minutes before serving, add the orzo and beans, adjust seasonings and simmer again. Garnish with cheese before serving.

Meal Inspiration

Tomato Curried Indian Chicken

Meal Inspiration

4 boneless chicken breasts

1 T. vegetable oil

10¾ oz. can tomato soup

½ c. plain yogurt (use Greek yogurt, if desired)

¼ c. water

¼ t. black pepper

⅛ t. cayenne pepper

2 t. curry powder

4 c. hot, cooked basmati rice

Sauté the chicken in the oil until browned on both sides, about 6 minutes. Add the soup, yogurt, water, peppers, and curry powder and blend well to combine. Cover and simmer for 20 minutes, or until the chicken is fully cooked. Serve the chicken and sauce over the rice.

Slow-Cooked Mushroom Chicken

SERVES 4

3-4 lbs. fryer chicken, cut into pieces

1 t. salt

1 t. black pepper

¼ t. ground paprika

1½ oz. dehydrated onion soup mix

10¾ oz. can cream of mushroom soup

¼ c. lowfat milk

4 oz. can sliced mushrooms, drained

2 oz. instant mashed potatoes, prepared

Preheat the oven to 350°F. Place the chicken in a 3-quart casserole and dust each piece with salt, pepper and paprika. Mix together the soups, milk and mushrooms and pour over the chicken. Bake for 2 hours, or until the chicken is tender and cooked through. Serve the chicken and sauce over the mashed potatoes.

Meatloaf with Spicy BBQ Sauce

SERVES 4 TO 6

1 lb. lean ground beef

1 small white onion, finely chopped

1 large egg

2 slices white bread, torn into small pieces

1 t. dried parsley

1 t. dried Italian seasoning

1 t. salt

½ t. black pepper

2 T. Worcestershire sauce

Spicy BBQ Sauce:

8 oz. can tomato sauce

1 T. prepared mustard

1 T. Worcestershire sauce

Preheat the oven to 375⁰F. In a large bowl, combine the beef, onion, egg, bread, parsley, Italian seasoning, salt, pepper and Worcestershire sauce. Mix lightly by hand. Form into a loaf shape and place in a 9 x 13-inch baking pan. Bake for 30 minutes. Mix together the tomato sauce, mustard and Worcestershire sauce in a small bowl. Pour over the meatloaf and continue baking for 30 minutes.

Creamy Chicken Broccoli Bake

2 10 oz. pkgs. frozen broccoli cuts, thawed, drained

4 oz. can sliced water chestnuts

8 oz. chicken breast, cubed

10¾ oz. can cream of celery soup

1 c. dry bread crumbs

¼ c. butter, melted

Preheat the oven to 350°F. Layer the broccoli and water chestnuts in a 1½-quart casserole. Place the chicken on top. Pour the soup over all and bake, covered, for 30 minutes. Uncover and top with the bread crumbs. Pour the butter over the crumbs and bake again for 15-20 minutes, or until chicken is cooked through completely.

Beef, Broccoli & Brown Rice Skillet

SERVES 4

½ lb. cooked deli roast beef, cut into matchstick pieces

1 t. freshly ground black pepper

10¾ oz. can cream of mushroom soup

2 c. instant brown rice

1 c. broccoli florets, cut into small pieces

In a skillet, heat the roast beef slices on medium heat and add the pepper. Stir and add the soup. Slowly add 1 soup can of water, rice and broccoli. Stir again and cook on medium-high heat until the mixture boils. Reduce heat to medium and cook without stirring for 5 minutes. Remove, let stand for 5 minutes before serving.

Pan-Fried Fish Fillets au Gratin

SERVES 4

1 lb. frozen fish fillets, thawed

½ c. Italian-style dried breadcrumbs

½ t. lemon pepper

½ c. mild cheddar cheese, shredded

5 oz. instant couscous, prepared, kept warm

Preheat the oven to 400°F. Coat a 9 x 9-inch baking pan with cooking spray. Place the fillets in the pan and cover with the breadcrumbs. Sprinkle the lemon pepper over all. Bake, uncovered, for 20-25 minutes. Top each fillet with cheese and continue baking for 5 minutes. Serve the fillets over the prepared couscous.

Vegetable Lo Mein

Meal Inspiration

1 T. canola oil

2 t. sesame oil, divided

8 oz. pkg coleslaw vegetables (cabbage mix)

1 c. mushrooms, sliced

1 c. bean sprouts

3 green onions, sliced

1 c. vegetable broth

Soy sauce to taste

8 oz. udon noodles

Heat the canola oil and 1 teaspoon sesame oil in a large sauté pan on high heat. Add the coleslaw mix and stir-fry for 3 minutes. Add the mushrooms, sprouts, onions and broth and stir-fry for 2 minutes. When tender-crisp, add soy sauce and noodles. Toss and fry until heated through.

Chicken Salsa Chili

SERVES 4

2 T. canola oil

8 oz. chicken meat, cubed

1½ c. frozen stir-fry vegetables

2 15 oz. cans small chili beans, with liquid

1 c. spicy salsa

1 c. tortilla chips, crushed

Heat the oil in a large saucepan on medium-high heat and add the chicken. Sauté on medium heat until cooked through, about 4 minutes. Add the vegetables, beans with liquid, and salsa and stir well. Continue cooking on medium-low heat for 10 minutes. Garnish with tortilla chips before serving.